# WHO LIVES IN A TROPICAL RAINFOREST?

## NATURE FOR KIDS

### Children's Nature Books

Speedy Publishing LLC
40 E. Main St. #1156
Newark, DE 19711
www.speedypublishing.com

The rainforests of Earth are warm, wet forests that grow in the warm band of the planet known as *"The Tropics"*. Who lives in the rainforests? Let's find out!

Mountainous Rain Forest Landscape Near Krabi In Thailand.

# LIVING
# IN THE
# RAINFOREST

You can find rainforests in South America, West Africa, southern India, Southeast Asia, and parts of Australia. They provide rich and complex environments for living creatures of all types. Residents of rainforests include people, animals, and insects.

Wooden houses on stilts along the Amazon river.

# RAINFOREST PEOPLE

Over 50 million people live in rainforests around the world. Many of them are part of tribes and cultures that live very much as they have lived for thousands of years. They get their food, shelter, clothing, and medicine from the rainforests.

Rainforest dwellers know how to use the riches of the forests without destroying the forests. They hunt and fish, gather fruit and nuts, and grow crops that can flourish on the forest floor. Most children of rainforest people do not go to formal schools. Instead, they learn techniques and traditions from their parents and tribal leaders.

*Indigenous Man Hunting in the Amazon.*

However, there is pressure on the rainforests from the outside world. People and companies want to cut down the trees for lumber, dig up the ground to find minerals, or build dams that drown valleys under water reservoirs. As the rainforests are cut down, the people who live in them have fewer resources to support their traditional way of life.

Jaguar in Brazilian Pantanal.

# RAINFOREST ANIMALS

Rainforests are home to a wide range of animals. In fact, the same area of rainforest can have completely different animal populations living on the forest floor, in the first layers of leafy branches, and in the forest canopy.

Here are some rainforest animals from different parts of the world:

## SOUTH AMERICA

Rainforest mammals include Jaguars, Ocelots, Opossums, Sloths, Capybaras, Peccaries, Howler Monkeys and Spider Monkeys.

Birds have wonderful names like Antbirds, Ovenbirds, Flycatchers, Quetzals, Macaws, Curassows, Hoatzins, Puffbirds, Toucans, Jacamars, Tanagers, Honeycreepers, and Xenops.

Reptiles include Anacondas, Iguanas, Boa Constrictors, Coral Snakes, Caimans, and a wide range of lizards.

There are amphibians like the Poison Arrow Frog. You don't want to meet him!

*Red poison dart frog.*

Fish include electric eels  and piranhas, along with many other species also found in other parts of the world.

## AUSTRALIA

Australian rainforest mammals include tree kangaroos and rat kangaroos, opossums, bandicoots, the Yellow-Footed Antechinus, the Duck-Billed Platypus, Sugar Gliders, and Red-Legged Pademelons.

*Toucan on the branch in tropical forest of Brazil.*

Among the birds are Cassowaries, Emerald Doves, Orange-Footed Scrubfowl, the Brolga, Sarus Cranes, Bush-Turkeys, Goshawks, Wompoo Fruit Doves, Topknot Pigeons, King Parrots, Kookaburras, The Lesser Sooty Owl, Fernwrens, and Golden Whistlers.

Reptiles particular to Australian rainforests include Carpet Pythons, Green Tree Snakes, Frilled Lizards, The Eastern Water Dragon, and the Northern Leaf-Tailed Gecko. There is a wide range of amphibians, including giant tree frogs, northern barred frogs, and striped marsh frogs.

*Southern Cassowary bird - Australia.*

# SOUTHEAST ASIA

Mammals in the rainforests include many kinds of primates, including Gibbons, Orangutans, and Colobine Monkeys; Tarsiers, Tigers, Tree Shrews, the Binturong, Moonrats, Flying Foxes, Colugos, and Bamboo Rats.

Among the birds are Leafbirds, Fairy Bluebirds, Fantails, Flowerpeckers, Wood Swallows, and Tree Swifts.

*Tarsier.*

# WEST AFRICA

Among the wide range of rainforest mammals are Bonobo, Chimpanzees, Gorillas, Mandrills, Scaly-Tailed Squirrels, Duikers, the Hippopotamus, Bushbabies, and Otter Shrews.

Birds unique to the African rainforest include African Gray Parrots and Congo peafowl.

*Mandrill.*

Redknee tarantula.

# RAINFOREST INSECTS

There are many more species of insects in the rainforests than there are of any other type of living creature. Some are very bright and beautiful, some are spiky and scary, and some use camouflage so it is hard to see them at all!

Most of the insects live high up in the trees, rather than down on the forest floor.

Insects in the rainforests play important roles in the life of the rainforest and all who live in it:

- **Source of food:** Insects provide food for many animals, from birds to bats to frogs to army ants. They even provide food for carnivorous plants! Read the Baby Professor book *Do Plants Eat Meat?* to learn more.

- **Restore the soil:** Some insects eat leaves and bark that trees shed. They break down the material into a form that can quickly decompose and become part of the soil, adding nutrients that the forest can re-use.

*Floor of the rainforest.*

- **Fertilize the plants:** Insects carry pollen from plant to plant, helping them fertilize each other so they can produce their seeds and fruit. Some plants rely on only one or two insect species to carry their pollen, so if those insects become extinct, the plants will be in serious trouble.

*Decaying timber filled by moss.*

# BUTTERFLIES

Rainforest butterflies are sometimes very large, and almost always very beautiful. You could choose your favorite from the Clear-Wing Butterfly, the Owl Butterfly, the Leaf-Wing Butterfly, and the Blue Morpho.

*Blue morpho butterfly.*

There is even a type of butterfly, the ithomiine, whose lifestyle is completely different from all other butterflies. Most butterflies do all their eating during their caterpillar stage, and then live off their food reserves during their butterfly stage. The ithomiine eats all through its life: its food is the droppings of the antbirds, who follow the long columns of army ants as they move through the rainforest floor. The army ants provide a constant, moving, food economy for the antbirds and the ithomiine butterflies!

Tropical beetle.

# BIG BUGS!

Although most insects in the rainforest are small, others are among the world's largest.

- Some tropical beetles may grow to six inches long.

- Centipedes can grow to eight inches long. Rainforest centipedes are carnivorous, and have poison claws underneath the main part of their body that they use to attack their prey.

On the other hand, rainforest scorpions are much smaller than their desert cousins.

# ANTS

There are many types of ants that live in the rainforests. Two of the most famous are the army ants of South America and the leafcutter ants in rainforests around the world.. They are not only interesting in the way they live, but in the way they contribute to the life of their rainforest home.

## THE ARMY ANTS

Army ants travel through the rainforest floor in a huge column of hundreds of thousands of ants.

*Camponotus gigas or giant forest ant.*

They eat as they go and carry their eggs and young ants with them in the center of the column, along with the queen. They are too many for insects or even small animals to fight, and army ants have been known to consume whole goats or cows that have been tied to a fence or a tree and can't run away.

Some people who live in the rainforest actually are happy when army ants pass through their village. The ants eat or drive away all sorts of pests, from small biting insects to rats and snakes.

The fighting force of the army ant column are soldier ants, very large, ferocious ants with powerful jaws. Most of the ants in the column are workers who are much smaller, though.

Many birds follow the army ants because other insects try to get away from the ant column. Insects that would normally stay hidden during the day, when the birds are hunting, fly up out of the way of the ants and into the path of the birds.

Army ants.

However, some wasps, beetles and other insects can emit a chemical "signature" like that of the army ants. This lets them move right along with the column of ants without danger to themselves, and lets them share in the feast when the ants find something good to eat. Most ants have very poor vision, so they have to trust their sense of smell.

*Leaf Cutter Ant army building a nest by using a leaf.*

## THE LEAFCUTTER ANTS

Leafcutter ants move in columns through tropical jungles, but their columns are smaller than those of the army ants. Large leafcutter ants move out from the nest in work teams to cut down suitable leaves and bring them back to the nest. As they travel along, carrying their leaves like huge banners, tiny leafcutter ants stand at the top of each leaf.

Their job is to protect the leaf from flies that lay their eggs in the leaves. If the larvae of these flies hatch inside the colony, they can damage the whole colony, or even kill it.

When the leafcutters bring their leaves home, they place them in a chamber as much as 20 feet underground. Smaller ants cut the leaves into smaller pieces. Then they take those pieces to another chamber, where even smaller ants chew the pieces into a paste. The ants use this leaf paste to feed fungus that the ants like to eat. Another bunch of leafcutter ants act as the farmers, taking care of the fungus!

*Leafcutter Ants.*

Even though the ants work so well together, there is no "brain" or smart central leader giving out orders. Each ant does the job that suits its size, age, and jaw strength.

Ants do communicate by sharing smells and sounds, but what they are sharing is information ("Good food is over there." "A wasp is attacking us!") not plans and orders.

*Leaf-cutter ant, Acromyrmex octospinosus, carrying a leaf.*

Fireflies flying around in the forest.

# FORESTS ALL AROUND US!

To learn more about Earth's forests, including rainforests, read Baby Professor books like *Ecosystem Facts That You Should Know - The Forests Edition.* Other Baby Professor books, like *Who Lives in the Barren Desert?,* tell you more about creatures living on other parts of our beautiful Earth.

Visit
BABY PROFESSOR
EDUCATION KIDS
www.BabyProfessorBooks.com
to download Free Baby Professor eBooks
and view our catalog of new and exciting
Children's Books